50 cool–girl quirks that prove there's
nothing crazy about loving cats

CRAZY
CAT
LADY

ALISON DAVIES

Hardie Grant

QUADRILLE

Enigmatic, alluring and almost always quirky, cats — and the ladies that love them — share much in common. As individual as their feline counterparts, crazy cat women exude charm, and while they have their eccentricities, they refuse to hide them. Instead, they take centre stage and celebrate what makes them unique: the bond between femme fatale and furry feline.

It's an age-old thing, an understanding born from intuition as much as superstition. For as women have been misunderstood over the years, so too have cats. Associated with witches and also cohorts of the devil, simply staring into a cat's eyes could transport hapless humans to the fairy otherworld.

Any cat-loving girl will attest the hypnotic appeal of her kitty's peepers is moggy magic at its finest, so it's easy to see where this comes from. And while some sneer at the general adoration cat ladies dish out to their beloved mog (along with the finest fresh salmon) those of us in the know understand that what we give out we get back in so many delightful ways. Yes, cat ladies go the extra mile when it comes to anything feline related. It's all part of the fun. On the surface we may be covered in a permanent layer of fur and scratches, but don't be fooled. We've found our purrfect.

If you've never experienced the joyful thrum of the purr, the just-as-lovable 'put-you-in-your-place' stare or the rich rewards of a tummy-tickling session, then I say to you, paws and pause before you judge.

So here's to all you feline-loving gals! This book is a celebration of your pawsomeness. And if you're on the fence when it comes to embracing your inner-cat craziness but recognise some of the 50 traits outlined in these pages, don't be shy. There's a reason you have this book in your hands!

Come join the party. It really is where all the cool cats hang out.

You can't get enough kitty print in your wardrobe.

Crazy Cat Lady – the clue is in the title.
If it's got a cat on it, it's yours, and anyway,
you can never own too many fleecy kitty
PJs or cute kitten slippers.

The grocery delivery driver remarks on the lack of human food in your shop.

Well, you have to cater for your kitty's discerning tastebuds, and that means several different types of feline fodder, not to mention the latest cat treats, biscuits, wine (yes wine – think 'pawsecco', 'cat-bernet sauvignon' or a rather fine 'miaow-bec').

One name isn't enough; you have *at least* six cute nicknames for your cat.

Little miss fluffy bunny head is a lady with many layers to her *purrsonality*. Move over Madonna, your moggy is the real queen of re-invention; a kitty diva with attitude.

Your cats have their own bedrooms (including your own).

Who needs a guest bedroom anyway? Much better that Captain Tiddles has the space to chillax. After all, it's hard work being perfect all day.

You no longer notice the cat hairs...

OK, so they're on the carpet, cushions,
table, kitchen surfaces, in the bath,
on your clothes and even in your tea.
Your feline keeps on giving!

Ms Boo Boo has her own Instagram and Twitter accounts...

...and numerous followers, with one thing in common – they're all crazy cat ladies too! Well a girl's got to have presence, and we're not talking gifts, although she has plenty of those too.

You shop online (even when you don't need to) for the cardboard delivery boxes.

Just in case your kitty takes a liking to one, at least for a day or two. Cat-loving girls know there's hours of fun to be had with a simple cardboard box.

The content of your camera roll is all cat.

You're a proud kitty mum.
It goes with the territory.

You think your cat understands you.

They do. They really do. They know exactly what you need at any given time: to adore, pamper and worship them.

Pacing the streets with a packet of cat treats is part of your nightly routine.

It's also a great way to keep fit.
All cats know this and encourage their
owners to take regular exercise by going
missing at the same time each evening.

You are no longer repulsed when a dead rodent turns up on your favourite chair.

OK, so as far as gifts go it's no box of chocolates, but you still thank them and take a pic to document their hunting prowess.

In the corner of every room there's a fluffy ball, woolly mouse or feathery toy (or all three).

It's kitty feng shui don't you know!

Cute babies and small children have no power over you, but show you a snoozing moggy and you're a gooey mess.

It's the whiskers and the little pink nose, and those soft squidgy paws... how can you resist?

Everyone knows that if there was a zombie apocalypse you'd save your cat first.

Life without cats is not an option. Ever. Although they've probably already hit the road as their feline supersenses knew what was happening before you did.

You try to outstare your cat on a regular basis.

Yes, it's futile when up against the dismissive stare of your moggy, but you try anyway. Plus, you're convinced your cat has mystical powers; hours spent gazing into its peepers will one day prove this truth.

Dr Doolittle has nothing on you; cat speak is your second language.

It's your secret superpower and you practise it whenever you cross paths with a creature of feline persuasion.

Everything stops at the stroke of the cat.

Cat o'clock is the only time that counts when there's a moggy in need of a stroke. It's the purrfect way to de-stress for both of you.

All your devices sport images of cats.

Screensavers, wallpapers – you name it – it's one gorgeous kitty fest.

Your cat gets more pressies at Christmas than the rest of your family and friends put together.

That's because they're not as difficult to buy for and you get as much joy browsing the latest outfits and toys as they do playing with them. Everyone's a winner!

Speaking of the festive season, there's nothing you enjoy more than dressing your moggy as Santa, complete with red and white bib, furry hat and green felt holly.

It's a great photo opportunity, and you can use it as an email round robin to wish all your friends and family a Miaow-y Christmas.

You think a 'cat–bag' is a great idea and have considered patenting it for future generations of crazy cat ladies.

Failing that, it's a great excuse to buy a bigger handbag. All you need then is a feline-friendly fleece lining to pop inside and a couple of cat treats. Job done.

In honour of big and small cats everywhere, you've taken the leopard print fashion phase to the extreme.

It's head-to-toe spots and then some.

Your kitty has more designer pieces in her wardrobe than you do.

The best deserves the best. End of.

Your kitchen shelves are groaning with cat mugs...

...and cups and plates, tea towels,
kitty-shaped salt and pepper pots, planters...
the list goes on. A girl can never have too
many cat accessories.

You're thinking of getting (or already have) a tattoo of your cat.

It might seem like a big step to those not in the kitty club, but why not? You know you'll never get sick of it and you'll be forever bonded, fur to flesh.

The Lion King is your favourite film.

Along with _The Aristocats, Oliver & Company, Puss in Boots_ and _The Cat in the Hat_. Any film with a cat as the central character is sure to make it onto your top-ten best movies list.

There's nothing more satisfying than a reading sesh with your learned feline.

OK, so you started reading the magazine by yourself, but your cat made it clear they wanted in by positioning themselves square on the page. It's their way of making the article a pawsome read! And let's be honest, you don't mind looking at them instead.

You know it's your bed, but you'll happily share it with your kitty.

It's not *really* sharing; you're happy with a sliver of space near the edge as long as your moggy is snuggled next to you.

There's no other noise in the world more delightful than your cat gently purring on your lap.

Enough said.

While you might fancy tuna niçoise salad for lunch, you'll happily forgo this — to treat your cat.

The pleading saucer eyes say their need is greater than yours. And anyway, sharing food with your kitty is where it's at. Cheese and biscuits for two, yes purrlease!

You treat cats the same as chocolates.

One is never enough!

Your fridge door is covered in cat-themed magnets.

Subliminal messaging at its finest:
see cat, think cat, open fridge, feed cat.

Your cat speaks to your soul.

Particularly at 4am when
it's howling for food.

The best massages come from your cat.

OK, so you realise that your feline miaow-seuse is just practising the common kitty behaviour of kneading, but you'll take it anyway. Truth be told, you prefer it to the human equivalent.

A night in with your kitty is preferable to a night out.

While it might not happen all the time, it's true to say that a cosy evening curled up with your furry friend really is the cat's whiskers, plus the purrfect pick-me-up after a stressful day.

**There are more cat beds
than cushions in your home.**

And the cushions you do have now
belong to the cat...

**Speaking of cushions, most
of them are cat-shaped
or have cute images of
cats on them.**

Who doesn't want to be cocooned by kitties
while they're snuggling up to the real thing?

Your cat always gets dinner served before you, your partner and any other random person that happens to be visiting.

It's a simple equation:
top cat = top of the food chain.

Your favourite superhero is Cat Woman.

Cool first name and she seriously rocks a Spandex catsuit.

Cat videos on YouTube are your go-to happy place.

Doesn't matter how many times you see them, they still make you smile.

There's nothing better than a head butt from your cat.

You'll even take a bottom in the face as a sign of affection. Others may think this a step too far, but it's a scientific fact that both are signs of appreciation and acceptance.

Conversations with your cat make the world a better place.

OK, so you don't fully understand each other – so what? Between woman and cat there is only one language... love (and possibly tuna?).

Your cat has its own cupboard full of grooming products, which to be fair, is more than you have.

Naturally, a feline must always look its best. Nothing spoils a selfie more than a bad case of bed head, an errant fur tangle or some goop in the eye.

If reincarnation exists, you've made it known you're coming back as a cat.

What's not to love? Sleep, eat, play, repeat! Not to mention the general adoration from your human, the ability to snooze at the drop of a hat and the glorious tummy tickles.

You no longer notice your arms are covered in scratches.

They are, after all, marks of love and worn with pride, as any cat mum will tell you!

You think cats in hats are cute, but draw the line at a kitty unicorn horn.

Let's not forget the ancient Egyptians believed cats were gods. Cats still believe this to be true, and so do you.

Your couch looks like it's been savaged by a wild animal.

Kittens have claws and they're not afraid to use them. Understandable when you consider they are predators priming their weapons. And anyway, nice furniture is for those with nothing more exciting in their life.

You celebrate your cat's birthday.

The date is marked on the calendar for all to see. On the day, your cherished kitty gets its fill of catnip treats, cards and even a special birthday dinner, while you raise a glass at the magnificence that is your moggy.

You wait for your cat to finish lazing on the keyboard even though you are in the middle of writing an email.

It might be annoying for some, but your tech-savvy cat just wants to get in on the act. And why not? They're entitled to splurge on eBay for the latest catnip goodies or play a game of stalk the mouse.

You're known in and around the neighbourhood as the 'crazy cat lady'.

Not only does this make you smile, you do everything in your power to maintain the reputation.

Ask a 'crazy cat lady' to explain why cats are where it's at and she will no doubt look at you with sympathy, for if you have to ask, then you are truly missing out.

You may think that it's the same of any pet owner, but the difference is cats cannot be claimed or possessed. They do not look to you for acceptance because they are their own mog. Queen or King Kitty, nothing matters except me, myself and I. This might sound stand-offish and somewhat selfish to the feline outsider, but it's born from an inherent need to survive, to journey through this world with their tail held high and a belly full of the tastiest morsels.

Cats are wild animals. Whether big or small, stalking the jungle or the kitchen table, they are primed and ready to unleash the *feral*. And there is the truth to end all truths, dangling before you like a catnip mouse. It's the reason why 'crazy cat lady' is not just an awesome title, it's the *business*. The bomb. The cat's pyjamas (should they wear them). For to walk (live, play, serve and be) with felines, is to walk on the wild side, to reconnect with nature and its finest specimen.

The ladies that love such beasts are joyful, vibrant, powerful women who realise that the creature clothed in fur and curled up on the sofa next to them is a tiger at heart. Primal, feral and fabulous, not to be underestimated and *not unlike themselves*. Catty may once have been considered tatty, but today the moggy mistress is an icon of sass, for she knows real class comes with four paws and a purr. As this book proves, it's time to reclaim the name and celebrate your feline–loving fate.

Join together, in flurry of fur and fabulousness.

You are awesome, crazy cat lady!

Publishing Director Sarah Lavelle
Editor Harriet Webster
Designer Emily Lapworth
Illustrator Jennifer Bouron
Head of Production Stephen Lang
Production Controller Katie Jarvis

Published in 2020 by Quadrille,
an imprint of Hardie Grant Publishing

Quadrille
52–54 Southwark Street
London SE1 1UN
quadrille.com

Cataloguing in Publication Data:
A catalogue record for this book
is available from the British Library.

Text © Alison Davies 2020
Illustrations © Jennifer Bouron 2020
Design © Quadrille 2020

ISBN 978 1 78713 555 0

Printed in China

MIX
Paper from
responsible sources
FSC® C020056